MAREK DUBIŃSKI

TOMASZ BASARABOWICZ

# KAISERLICHE UND KÖNIGLICHE EISENBAHN-BAU KOMPANIE

## In Western Galicia 1914–1915

vol. 2

STRATUS

Published in Poland in 2019
by Wydawnictwo Stratus sp.j.
Po. Box 123,
27-600 Sandomierz 1, Poland
e-mail: office@wydawnictwostratus.pl

as
MMPBooks
e-mail: office@mmpbooks.biz



www.mmpbooks.biz
www.wydawnictwostratus.pl



**ISBN**
**978-83-65958-34-1**

*Editor in chief*
**Roger Wallsgrove**

*Editorial Team*
**Bartłomiej Belcarz**
**Robert Pęczkowski**
**Artur Juszczak**

*Cover*
**Dariusz Grzywacz**

*Book layout*
**Dariusz Grzywacz**

*Maps*
**Dariusz Karnas**

*Proofreading*
**Peter Brown**

**All photos: Marek Dubiński collection except stated**

*DTP*
**Bartłomiej Belcarz**

**PRINTED IN POLAND**

# General Outline of Military Operations in Western Galicia between August 1914 and mid-Summer 1915

The most intensive fighting commenced on 23rd August 1914 and ended – despite initial success – with the defeat of the Austro-Hungarian troops, who had to withdraw from most of the crownlands of Galicia. The Russian 3rd Army under General of Infantry Nikolai Russki managed by 2nd September to occupy the entirety of north-eastern Galicia, including the Galician capital city of Lwów/Lviv/Lemberg. Meanwhile, the Russian 8th Army, led by General of Cavalry Brusilov, captured the towns of Brody, Tarnopol, and Buczacz (all now in Ukraine) north of the River Dniester, and occupied most of Bukovina.

Even before the outbreak of war there had been German-Austrian agreements that armies of both states would forestall a strategic Russian offensive by rapid counterattacks. These were to be performed by the Germans in the north from East Prussia in the direction of River Narew and in the south – by the Austro-Hungarians – from Galicia in the direction of the Russian partition of Poland, thus lifting the axis of the dreaded "Russian steamroller" before the Russians could roll forward with their huge numerical superiority toward Silesia and Hungary. The Austro-Hungarian chief of staff Franz Conrad von Hötzendorf hoped that the German army would support him in the offensive in Galicia, but he was disappointed that only one German *Landwehrkorps* under General Remus von Woyrsch could be sent to the Kielce area as the primary supporting force to the River Vistula front. The connection with Silesia was secured by *Landwehr* formations, which covered the western bank of the Vistula River between Kielce and Sandomierz, forming the Army Group of General of Infantry Heinrich Kummer von Falkenfeld.

While the Germans were preparing for the defence of East Prussia, the Austro-Hungarian Chief-of-Staff Conrad von Hötzendorf decided to let the multinational army of Austria-Hungary take part in their offensive in Galicia with 37 divisions on a 400-kilometre-wide front:

In the north, the *k.u.k.* 1st Army under General Dankl between the River San and Vistula and to the right of it the *k.u.k.* 4st Army advancing in the direction of Brest-Litovsk, thus cutting off the strategic railway route from Kiev to Warsaw.

In Eastern Galicia, the *k.u.k.* 3rd Army under General of Cavalry Rudolf Brudermann covering Lwów/Lviv/Lemberg was to move against Brody, to the south Army Group "Kövess" should cover the line extending from Lwów/Lviv/Lember, the capital of Galicia, down to the River Dniester at Halicz and the area around Stanisławów/Stanislau (today Ivano-Frankivsk in Ukraine). Bukovina was secured by weak *Landwehr* formations.

An Austro-Hungarian Fross-Büssing adapted for use on the railway tracks.

Geographical location of the sites and places described in this volume.

At the same time, the Commander of the Russian Southwest Front, General of Artillery Nikolai Iudovich Ivanov, concentrated two of his armies (the 3rd and 8th Army) against Lwów/Lviv/Lemberg. In total, Ivanov led 53 infantry and 18 cavalry divisions to conquer Galicia from the east – the 8th Army deployed between Stanisławów/Stanislau and Tarnopol (today Ternopil in Ukraine) and the 3rd Army at the Dubno area. The remaining two Russian armies were to advance from the northeast, from the Lublin area. The General Quartermaster of the STAVKA General Danilov however demanded one combined attack southwest directly on Lwów/Lviv/Lemberg.

Although this double operation was to disperse Russian forces, General Ivanov was well-informed about the operational and deployment plans of Austria-Hungary by Colonel Redl – a Russian spy – and expected the main forces of the enemy near the city of Lwów/Lviv/Lemberg. The speed of the Russian march was completely ignored by the Austro-Hungarian leadership. The terrain conditions also favoured the attackers. The mountain rivers flowing down from the Carpathian Mountains – Wisłoka, San and Dniester – ran across the front lines and did not hinder the movements of the Russians.

When the Austro-Hungarian frontline had been broken, the *k.u.k.* troops withdrew, sometimes fleeing. Many of the Slavic-origin soldiers, especially the Czechs, surrendered without a fight and even offered to fight for the Russians. A total of 130,000 POWs were brought in by the Russians by 11 September, and total Austro-Hungarian losses in this fighting, later to be known as the Battle of Galicia, rose to 324,000. The Russians themselves suffered 225,000 casualties, plus 40,000 POWs. They were able to advance about 160 km to the River San, and it was on 16th September when for the first time they besieged the fortress of Przemyśl. The battle severely damaged the Austro-Hungarian army, destroying a large part of the officer corps. An important region of Austria-Hungary was temporarily lost. The *k.u.k.* Army on the Eastern Front could not recover from their defeat – it had lost a third of the officer corps and some of the best formations. Although the Russians had been defeated by the Germans at the Battle of Tannenberg, their victory in the Battle of Galicia significantly diminished the force of the German impact.

Next, "the Russian steamroller" moved west via Rzeszów and Tarnów and in late-1914 reached the fortress of Kraków.

After the severe military defeats of the first months of the war, the Danube Monarchy faced serious danger. Galicia was largely conquered by Russian troops, they were able to penetrate deep into the Carpathians. Even the German ally expressed dissatisfaction with the previous Austrian achievements compared to the Battle of Tannenberg.

The mountainous landscape of the Carpathians still provided a bad starting point for a Russian offensive in winter. However, this situation would change with the snowmelt, and in the event of a Russian breakthrough, the road was open to the Hungarian lowlands and plains and thus to a core area of the fragile multinational state.

In addition, on the other side of the mountains there was the isolated Austro-Hungarian fortress of Przemyśl with almost 150,000 troops under Russian siege. The efforts of the Central Powers played into the hands of the indecision of the Russian generals. On the one hand, an advance through the Carpathians into the Hungarian lowlands was possible. On the other hand, the comparatively better starting position in Galicia toward the Kraków area came into consideration as the basis for a possible attack further west against Silesia. Carrying the war onto German territory was a major demand by the Western Allies of the Tsarist empire. It was decided to pursue the latter option and to continue the offensive south of Kraków in order to get a better starting position against German territory itself.

At the beginning of December 1914, Conrad von Hötzendorf made an attempt to stop the impending disaster to the Austrian army. The Commander-in-Chief of the Russian Southwest Front, General Ivanov, prepared the attack of his 3rd Army (General Dimitriev) on Kraków, but this army was suddenly defeated by the depleted *k.u.k.* 4th Army which attacked in the area of Nowy Sącz in the gap between the flanks of the Russian 3rd Army under Dimitriev and the 8th Army under Brusilov, and here in December the Battle of Limanowa-Łapanów began. On either side of Łapanów there was a thirty-kilometre-wide frontline, which was only weakly secured by the Russian 9th Corps. The Austro-Hungarian Supreme Commander Joseph Ferdinand succeeded in deploying the *k.u.k.* 14th Corps unnoticed against the weak point of the opponent. The element of surprise was used and a flank "kick" against the Russian forces ended successfully.

The Austro-Hungarians pushed the Russian front about sixty kilometres to the northeast, but the Russians were able to quickly bring up their reserves and consolidate the front within a week. On 14 December, the advance of Conrad von Hötzendorf was over. By 28 December the Russian 8th Army had thrown the Austro-Hungarian 3rd Army under General Svetozar Boroević back to its starting line of the beginning of the month.

The main threat to the Hungarian plains from the Carpathians was still not resolved, neither was the problem of supplying the fortress of Przemyśl which was threatened with collapse due to lack of food and ammunition. In the

The railway station in Dębica as seen by the *k.u.k.* airmen of *Flik 10* squadron. (Muzeum Regionalne Dębica coll.)

area of the fortress itself, the *k.u.k.* troops were able to achieve minor tactical successes and position improvements during the previous battle. Conrad von Hötzendorf therefore planned an all-out offensive operation in the winter to relieve the fortress. He decided on an offensive on a broader front in the entire mountainous front.

The first offensive of the 3rd Army began on 23rd January 1915, and the operation did not go according to plan from the very beginning. The only success was to the easternmost group of troops, although the offensive in the west should have been the focus. The terrain gains were of little help, with the extended front and supply of the advanced troops devouring more resources than the previous favourable defensive positions in the mountains.

The Russian 8th Army, for its part, began a counter-offensive with the 12th Corps, which pushed the *k.u.k.* 7th Corps back to the Dukla Pass. The main Austro-Hungarian attacking force had been strengthened by two divisions withdrawn from the Serbian front, but still could not achieve success. The freezing weather and poorly scheduled operations led to high losses.

The first phase of the fighting, which had been going on since 8th December, cost the Austro-Hungarian armed forces 94,500 men by the end of January, of which over 61,000 were sick and wounded.

Between 27th February and 14th March, the second offensive took place after a desperate call for help from the fortress by Przemyśl's officer commanding, Hermann Kusmanek. The *k.u.k.* 2nd Army under General von Böhm-Ermolli was after four months ordered back to Galicia. The front of the 2nd Army established on 20th February on the eastern flank of the 3rd Army between the Łupków – Cisna area to Humenne. By the end of February, further reinforcements from Serbia arrived.

On 27th February the *k.u.k.* Corps Group of General of Cavalry Tersztyánszky breeched a twelve kilometres wide gap toward Baligród. The Russian resistance now led by General of Infantry Selivanov halted the *k.u.k.* troops on the line between Wetlina to Konieczna. By mid-March all Austro-Hungarian operations ended in a complete standstill.

These defeats were followed by an even more painful disaster – the surrender of the fortress of Przemyśl. The offensive in the Carpathians had since 8 December 1914 cost the Austro-Hungarian army almost 250,000 troops. Also, 88,000 wounded and sick men had been sent home and had to be replaced. These enormous losses hit the Danube Monarchy twice as hard. The frontline Austrian, German and Hungarian officers were over-represented in numbers, when compared to the proportions of all nationalities of the Empire. As a result, the core countries of the Monarchy had been required to pay the heaviest toll right from the start. The army of the multi-ethnic state lost more and more of its fighting power, and the winter offensives were supposed to be the last in the Great War – apart from the 1916 South Tirol offensive – carried out without significant assistance from the German ally.

On the Eastern Front a further effort by the Central Powers was necessary. Now, German troops had to be withdrawn from the Western Front on a large scale. A new German army, the 11th, was formed for the operation. The offensive began in May 1915 under August von Mackensen, with the Battle of Gorlice-Tarnów, which was already completely under German leadership.

It took place between the city of Tarnów and town of Gorlice, in the heart of Western Galicia. It marked the turning point on the Eastern Front. As a result, the Danube Monarchy was relieved of pressure from Russian armies. In the subsequent offensive on 22nd June 1915 Lwów/Lviv/Lemberg, the capital of Galicia, was recaptured.

Operational goal of the German 11th Army was to be between the flanks of the 9th and 10th Corps of the Russian 3rd Army to drive a wedge and throw back the northern flank of this army on Jarosław and the southern flank on the Carpathian front held back the *k.u.k.* 3rd and 2nd Armies which were to advance and complete the encirclement of the Russians. In the further course of the main thrust the River San was to be reached and by threatening the rear lines of the Russian 8th Army under Alexei Brusilov the Russian southwest front would be forced to abandon their positions in the area of Łupków and the Ushok Pass.

The terrain conditions favoured the operation: the flanks of the attacking units were covered in the north by the Vistula River, in the south by the Beskidy Mountains, and the existing railway network facilitated approach and supply. However, the problem was that the numerous Vistula tributaries running transversely to the axis of advance attack south-north direction had to be crossed and the network of routes in the area of operation consisted of only a few major roads. Army Group Mackensen consisted of the German 11th Army in the centre, the *k.u.k.* 4th Army on the northern flank and the *k.u.k.* 3rd Army subordinated to the southern flank forces.

South of the Vistula River along the River Dunajec, there was the *k.u.k.* 4th Army under Archduke Joseph Ferdinand with eight infantry divisions, a cavalry division and 253 guns, which was to attack towards Tarnów.

The main thrust in the centre was led by the German 11th Army (August von Mackensen) on the River Biała between Tuchów and Grybów with ten infantry divisions – 216,000 men and 634 guns – in the direction of Gorlice.

The *k.u.k.* 3rd Army (Svetozar Boroević) was to participate in the offensive after the initial breakthrough from its positions down south in the Beskidy Mountains between the Dukla Pass and Sztropko with ten infantry and two cavalry divisions.

The offensive commenced on 2nd May at 0600 hrs and ended with a total success. The details of how many troops were killed, wounded or taken prisoner in the Battle of Gorlice-Tarnóware – as in all battles of World War One – are inaccurate, incomplete and contradictory. What is certain is that the Russian losses were much higher than those on the German and Austro-Hungarian sides combined. One of the claims that there had been 820,000 casualties and 895,000 POWs on the Russian side, apparently refers not only to the Battle of Gorlice-Tarnów but to the Russian

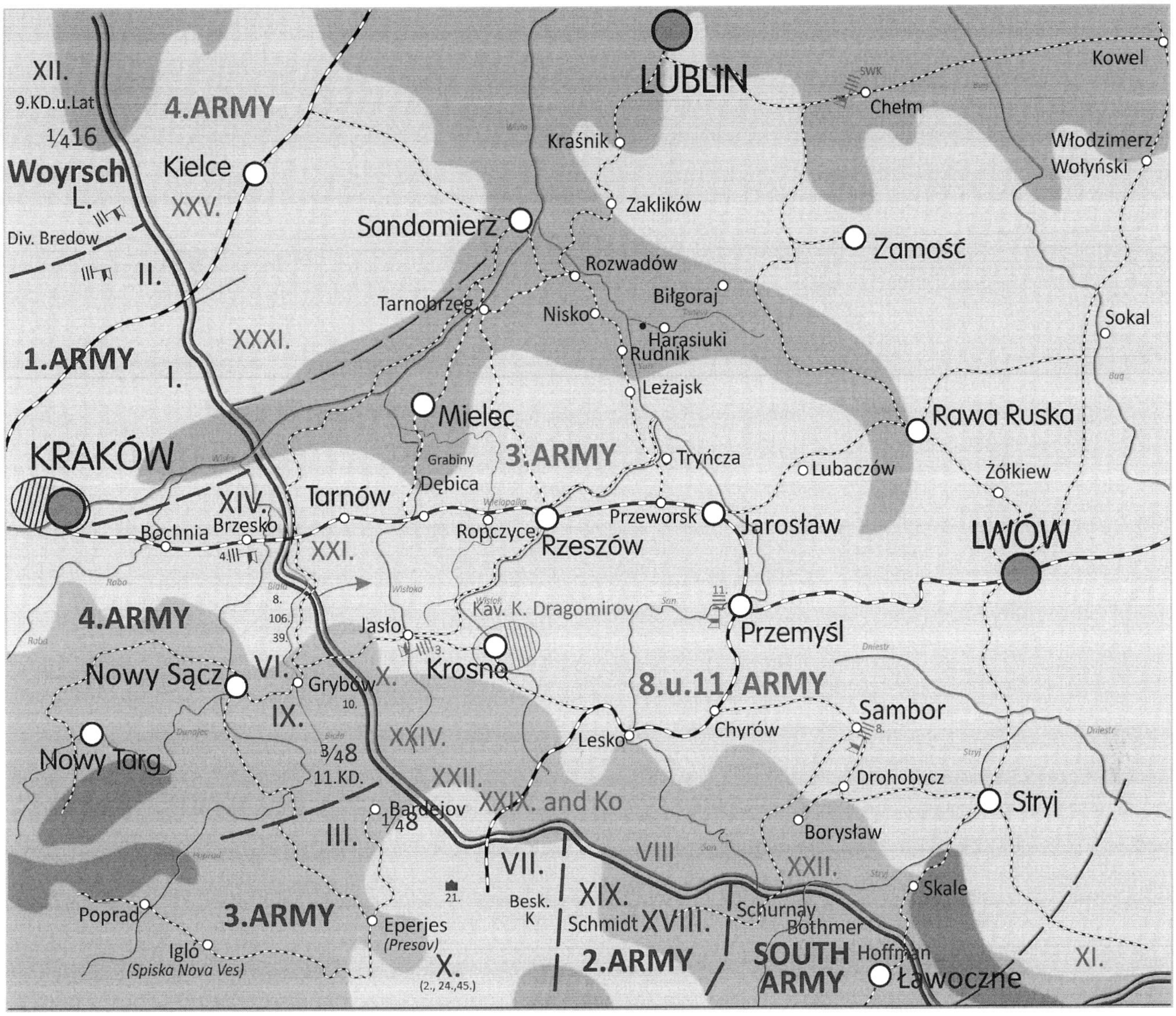


Galician front on 14th April 1915.

front from May to July 1915 as a whole. A German army report of 13th May 1915 mentions 143,000 Russian POWs. The Austro-Hungarian report of 12th May 1915 estimates Russian losses of at least 150,000 men, of which 100,000 were POWs. One of the references puts the Russian losses at "nearly 250,000 men" without distinguishing between dead, wounded and POWs. Richard DiNardo, who has produced the most detailed study to date of the Battle of Gorlice-Tarnów, estimates that up to 250,000 Russian troops were captured and more than 100,000 fell or were wounded.

The Battle of Gorlice-Tarnów was the decisive one for the Central Powers. The entire Carpathian front was lifted from its hinges, on 3rd/4th June the fortress of Przemyśl was re-taken, which the Russians had only captured on 22nd March. The Russians had to withdraw by about 100 km onto an unprepared line on the River San. The STAVKA tried to defend it with the remnants of the 3rd Army. Grand Duke Nikolai Nikolayevich said of them: *...barely trained peasant serfs, they have not even learned how to shoot properly...* On 14th June another 15,000 men surrendered. On 22nd June the city of Lwów/Lviv/Lemberg was reconquered. In these battles the Russian army lost more troops than it had lost in the Battle of Gorlice-Tarnów.

In the face of total defeat, the Russian leadership under Grand Duke Nikolai ordered the evacuation of Polish territory on 17th June, culminating in the "Great Retreat". The intention of the Western Allies to carry the war onto German territory became illusory. For the Central Powers, however, the operation was a complete success. The situation also eased for Austria-Hungary. The Dual Monarchy was now able to turn its attention almost entirely to the danger posed in the south by Italy as the new member of the Entente.

As for the Polish cause, with the fall of the Russian-held so called "Kingdom of Poland" to the Central Powers, the situation changed radically. The pro-Russian faction under Roman Dmowski was marginalised while the pro-Austrian side with 20,000 strong Polish Legions under Józef Piłsudski was strengthened.

Railway bridge over the River Wisłok in Rzeszów rebuilt by the *2. Eisenbahn-bau Kompanie* (2nd Railway Construction Company), October 1914. The original bridge was undermined by water during flooding on 5th–6th October and eventually collapsed. Note elements of the Kohn bridging system which can be seen in the upper left part of the image.

# RZESZÓW

The bridge shown on the previous page photographed from a different angle, October 1914. Pay attention to how the Kohn's span joins the original bridge's span on a pillar. Note also the wooden supporting structure underneath the Kohn bridging system.

Commanding officer of the *2. Eisenbahn-bau Kompanie*, Captain Viktor Mueller, Ritter von Elblein, Autumn 1914.

The *2. Eisenbahn-bau Kompanie* managed to rebuild the bridge between 11th and 17th of October 1914. The span built with the Kohn bridging system was 42 metres in length. Note the way in which the collapsed span of the original bridge acts as a foundation for the wooden supporting structure. A 200 metre-long bypass track had to be constructed as well.

A water tower in Rzeszów, May 1915. On the left the front part of a *kkStB 151* series locomotive can be seen.

A span of the street viaduct over the Rzeszów railway station tracks is being lifted and underpinned, May 1915.

**Top left:** A destroyed railway bridge over the River Wisłok in Rzeszów, May 1915. It was eventually rebuilt by the Austro-Hungarian *2.* and *24. Eisenbahn Kompanien* as well as the German *E.B.K. 4* and *27*.

**Top right:** A destroyed Russian field bridge in Rzeszów, May 1915. It was built with the outdated Eiffel bridging system which had also been used by the Austro-Hungarian engineers before the Kohn system was introduced.

A destroyed railway bridge over the River Wisłok in Rzeszów, May 1915. It was eventually rebuilt by the Austro-Hungarian *2.* and *24. Eisenbahn Kompanien* as well as the German *E.B.K. 4.* and *27*.

**Top left:** The first stages of construction of the new railway bridge over the River Wisłok in Rzeszów, May 1915. It was of mixed wooden and Kohn system construction and was located just beside the remnants of the original bridge. The basic elements of the wooden supporting structure are being erected. Note two pile drivers at work, both of them steam operated.

**Top right:** A general view of the new mixed construction bridge as of May 1915. Note the complicated system of supporting structures and cantilever beams. The elements of the Kohn system can be seen in the centre. The remains of the Russian Eiffel system bridge are visible on the left in the background.

The new bridge was built in just five and a half days, from 25th to 30th May 1915. Total length of the new bridge was 72 metres, while the spans alone were 59 metres long. Note a *kkStB 73* series locomotive and timber-laden platform wagons performing the endurance trial.

**Right:** The endurance tests of 30th May 1915 from another perspective. Note the black-yellow flag of the Danube Monarchy flying in the centre and the red-white-red German flag on the extreme right. The inscription on the commemorative plate placed between both flags says it is the *Bundesbrücke* (Union Bridge). Written below, we can also see the names of the Austro-Hungarian and German engineer units which were responsible for the bridge construction – the *E.B.K. 4.* and *27.*, as well as the *2.* and *24. Eisenbahnkompanien.*

The ultimate endurance trial of the newly-built bridge over the River Wisłok in Rzeszów, 30th May 1915. Note the *kkStB 73* series locomotive and fully-laden wagons. There is a roll call of the engineers on the left of the image and the footbridge to the right as well as more engineers on the extreme right. Rzeszów railway station is located further to the left, that is westwards.

**Left:** Two officers from the units which built the bridge – an Austro-Hungarian and a German. The original caption reads *Leutenant Kühne and I.* The photograph comes from the archive of the *E.B.K. 4.*, hence we can guess Kühne belonged to this unit.

**Right:** A souvenir photograph of a group of Austrian and German officers taken after the bridge over the River Wisłok had been completed on 30th May 1915. The original caption reads *Muli, Stefenson, I, Kühne, Kerzendacht.*

**Bottom:** For the Germans the bridge was also known as the *Elefanten-Brücke* (Elephant Bridge). Here German engineers of the *E.B.K. 27.* pose for a photograph with a handful of their Austro-Hungarian colleagues to the right and under the bridge, Rzeszów, May 1915.

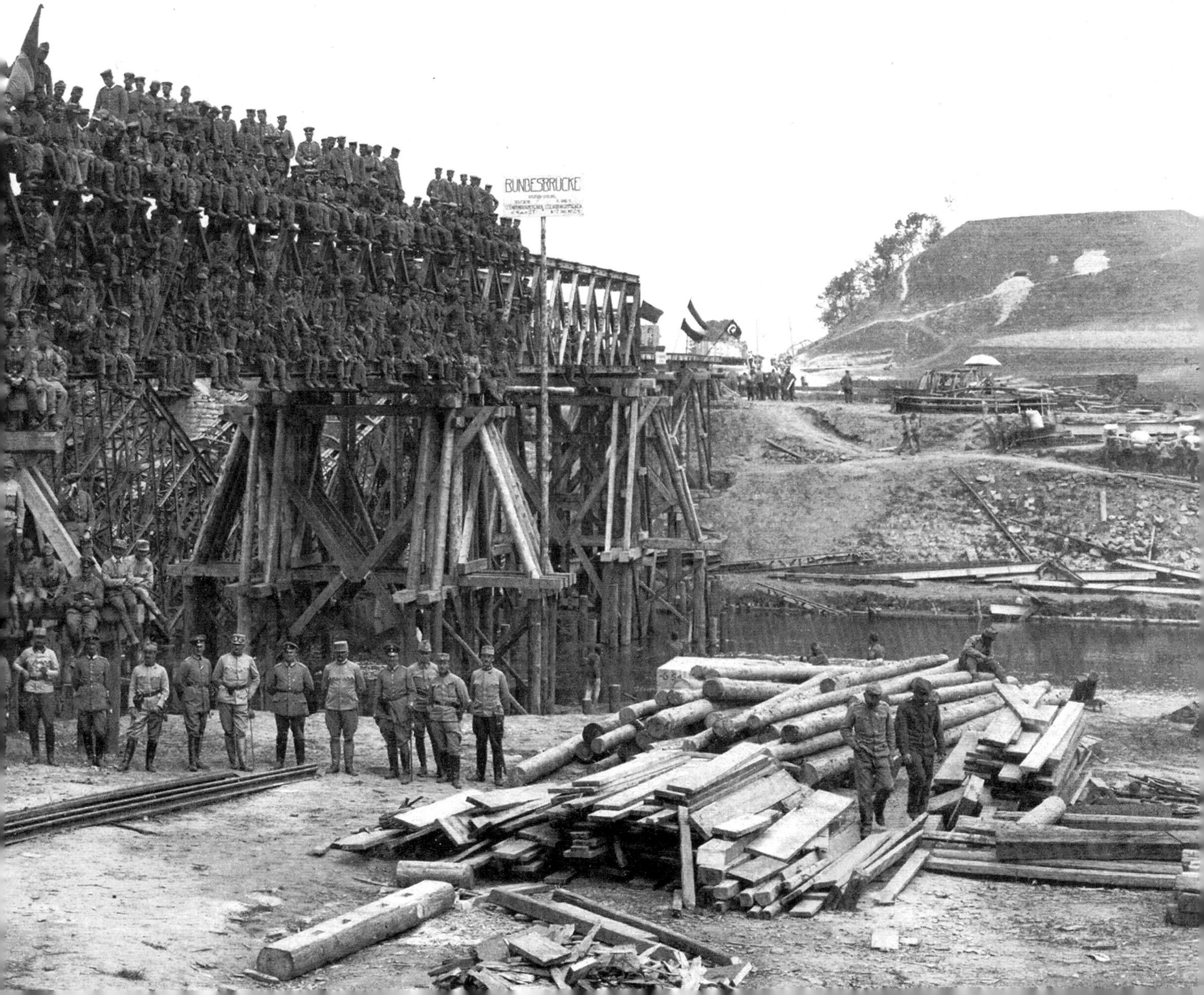
BUNDESBRÜCKE

German engineers of the *E.B.K. 27.* re-built another bridge over the River Wisłok near Rzeszów in May 1915. To construct the upstream one-track span took them seven days. They worked with their own Roth-Wagner bridging system which was better and easier to assemble than the Austro-Hungarian Kohn type. The Roth-Wagner span was 8.45 m above the riverbed. Note how a stack of timber for railway sleepers is being used to support the structure.

A diver tries to determine how much the river bottom of Wisłok was littered with remnants of the demolished bridge, May 1915. He is being observed and secured by German railway engineers.

The process of disassembling what had been left of the Russian field bridge of the Eiffel system. Rzeszów, May 1915. Note the concrete structure of the original bridgehead pillar.

Three close-up views of the Eiffel bridging system. It was still used by the Tsarist engineers in those days, although it had long been declared obsolete by the *k.u.k.* troops and replaced by the Kohn system. Note the means of assembly of the Eiffel system.

# PRZEWORSK

Railway bridge over the Mleczka stream near Przeworsk, Autumn 1914. It was built by the *12. Eisenbahnkompanie* from elements of the damaged original girder span, which was strengthened with timber and planks, and a short improvised section of wood-based track.

The same bridge seen from the other side, Autumn 1914. The image clearly demonstrates the way the track was laid on the wooden base and supported by a wooden construction by engineers of the *12. Eisenbahnkompanie* (originally spelled "12. Eisenbahn-Kompagne"), and how is it connected to the stone bridgehead. Note the second of the twin single-track spans in the background which collapsed completely after it had been demolished by Russian troops during their retreat in the first stage of the Battle for Galicia.

A close-up view of the first wooden strengthening of the damaged span of the bridge over the Mleczka stream, Autumn 1914.

**Right:** Another bridge on the very same route which was located in Ruda-Sarcina had to be repaired twice by the *k.u.k.* railway engineers. The first time was in October 1914 by the *2. Eisenbahnkompanie* after the Tsarist forces had been pushed north-east during the Battle for Galicia. For the second time, when it was re-captured during the successful offensive of May/June 1915 and rebuilt by the *24. Eisenbahnkompanie*. The photograph was taken after engineers of the latter unit had completed their task.

Both single-track spans of the bridge over the Mleczka stream near Przeworsk after one of them had been repaired by the *k.u.k. 12. Eisenbahnkompanie* in the Autumn of 1914. The original bridges were part of the important Przeworsk-Nisko railway route.

182

# RUDA NEAR NISKO

This was a clear example how the *k.u.k.* railway engineers were able to rebuild a bridge even when specialist equipment was not available, June 1915. Elements of the original span were used and here we can see a middle part of it prepared for lifting. The remaining two had already been raised and supported by stacks of railway sleeper timber.

Railway bridge on the Przeworsk-Nisko route, blown up by the withdrawing Tsarist troops. The photograph was taken on 15th June 1915, shortly after it had been captured.

# TRYŃCZA

A narrow-gauge field railway station at Tryńcza, June 1915. It was a terminus of the tracks, which look like they had been laid in haste. On the right a casualty clearing post can be seen.

Austro-Hungarian railway engineers of an unidentified unit loading beams onto narrow-gauge platform wagons, June 1915.

Food supplies distributed among the railway engineers at Tryńcza, June 1915. In the background three rows of narrow-gauge platforms can be seen.

At the Tryńcza station, June 1915. Note a small railway cart on the right and the horse-drawn wagon in the background.

A long narrow-gauge train prepared to move, June 1915. Pay attention to the way the load of barrels was secured by beams.

A horse-drawn narrow-gauge field kitchen wagon at Tryńcza. See the small trolley on the right.

REPARATURS-WERKSTATTE

Another look at the horse-drawn railway field kitchen, June 1915. The inscription on the board informs us that we are at kilometre zero of the narrow-gauge track at Tryńcza. On the left a part of the field workshop is visible.

A horse-drawn man-carrying wagon, June 1915. Strangely enough it was equipped with comfortable chairs. The now-familiar workshop building can be seen to the left.

**Left:** The field railway workshop in Tryńcza, June 1915. The building was constructed with wicker. Over the entrance *Reparaturs Werkstätte* is written. Note also the wagon bogies.

The *k.u.k.* railway engineers lifting a girder of the Eiffel bridging system in order to support a span of the railway bridge in Tryńcza, June 1915. The first elements of the wooden supporting structure are also in place already. Note a stack of sleepers on the right as well as part of a pile driver visible in the background.

The stack of sleepers from the image on the previous page is now replaced by an Eiffel bridging system girder supporting the middle span of the same system, June 1915. The original wooden support structure had been burnt. The photograph was taken during the endurance trials, when – as usual – a fully-laden train was used to check the quality of the engineers' work.

A train rolls onto the now completed bridge over River Wisłok in Tryńcza, June 1915. The middle Eiffel system span was 42 metres long. Both original bridge spans can also be seen.

# LEŻAJSK AREA

A direct hit of an artillery round on the railway station in Leżajsk, Battle for Galicia, October 1914. The town was captured by a battalion of the 77th Infantry Regiment. Note the Russian railway engineers had already managed to widen the rail spacing into their own 1,524 mm gauge.

The town of Sieniawa located at the Tarnogród-Tryńcza field narrow-gauge railway, June 1915.

Barrack of the *2. Eisenbahnkompanie* in Cieplice on the narrow-gauge line, June 1915. Note a train drawn by a handcar on the right.

To make the ride more comfortable some parts of the field railway were laid on sleepers, June 1915. We can see four horses drawing a narrow-gauge platform laden with sleepers at Cieplice.

Horse replacement post in Cieplice, June 1915. The crate-carrying platforms as well as the empty ones on the right are protected with beams from bumping up against each other.

# HARASIUKI AREA

The narrow-gauge field railway route Harasiuki-Janów, June 1915.

The field railway station in Harasiuki, June 1915.

A camp of the railway engineers responsible for maintaining and operating the field railway, June 1915.

Just before Janów the transports of the railway route had to run on an old and poor Russian road as the area around was swampy, June 1915.

A small bridge at Kusze, built on the Tryńcza-Tarnogród route by the *2. Eisenbahnkompanie* in June 1915.

So-called *Honved-Platz* in June 1915. The name of the place may suggest some of the troops listening to the music are Hungarian. In the distance a line of requisitioned local horse-drawn carts carrying supplies on a road which was commonly known as *Końska Ulica* or "Horse Street" in Polish

# RUDNIK

Eighty per cent of the town of Rudnik's buildings were in ruins in June 1915.

Very interesting image depicting a temporary crossing over the River Tanew in the foreground, on which narrow-gauge tracks and horse-drawn platforms can also be seen, June 1915. Just behind it engineers are at work on a much larger bridge, which would not be prone to potential flooding. We can see as many as eight manually operated pile drivers. In the background a completed ramp running to a bridgehead and resting on the wooden supports is clearly visible.

This photograph was taken at the same spot, after the bridge had been completed. It is of entirely wooden construction and the field railway tracks are now transferred onto the larger crossing. The temporary one would soon be dismantled.

An original tiny building of the Rudnik railway station, June 1915. Major Junk, on the right, mounted, is inspecting the railway engineers responsible for traffic operations.

Railway engineers at work on an extension of the narrow-gauge track network at the Rudnik station, June 1915.

Construction material is being unloaded from a normal-gauge train at the station of Rudnik, June 1915. Note two types of the *kkStB* open goods wagons.

Railway construction material was unloaded directly onto narrow-gauge platforms by means of makeshift ramps, Rudnik, June 1915.

Engineers laying the normal-gauge field railway tracks at Rudnik in early Summer of 1915. Such tracks could be quickly and easily dismantled.

A narrow-gauge field railway station in the village of Kamionka near Rudnik, Summer 1915. We can see pre-assembled segments of the narrow-gauge tracks.

# NISKO AREA

Railway engineers' post in Nisko, 15th June 1915.

On 15th June 1915 the Russians shelled the railway engineers' post in Nisko. As a result one officer (Captain Elemer Illcs) and three other ranks died.

The narrow-gauge field railway tracks just before Janów having been laid on deep sand, Summer 1915.

Positions of the *k.u.k.* railway engineers in the near vicinity of the Rozwadów-Nisko route in Summer 1915. The tracks laid in this sandy area as well as the amount of traffic required constant checking.

A small bridge on the Dębica-Nisko railway route near the village of Dąbie, June 1915. We can see German railway engineers of the *E.B.K. 7.* at work. The collapsed span was raised step by step with layers of railway sleepers.

204

Another, larger railway bridge on the Dębica-Nisko route at Dąbie, demolished by the retreating Tsarist troops in late May or early June 1915. This time engineers of the German *E.B.K. 7.* did not bother with lifting the blown-up span. Instead, they built a wooden bypass crossing.

Re-building of the small bridge at Dąbie, June 1915. Note the span had already been levelled and is now supported by a stack of sleepers. The German engineers of the *E.B.K. 7.* are working on a connection between the damaged span and opposite bridgehead. Note two hand-operated pile drivers.

Once the job is done, it is the time for the endurance trial. The popular *kkStB 73* series locomotive was the obvious choice.

This hotel in Rozwadów photographed in June 1914, shortly before the outbreak of The Great War, was the quarters of the *k.u.k.* railway engineer officers

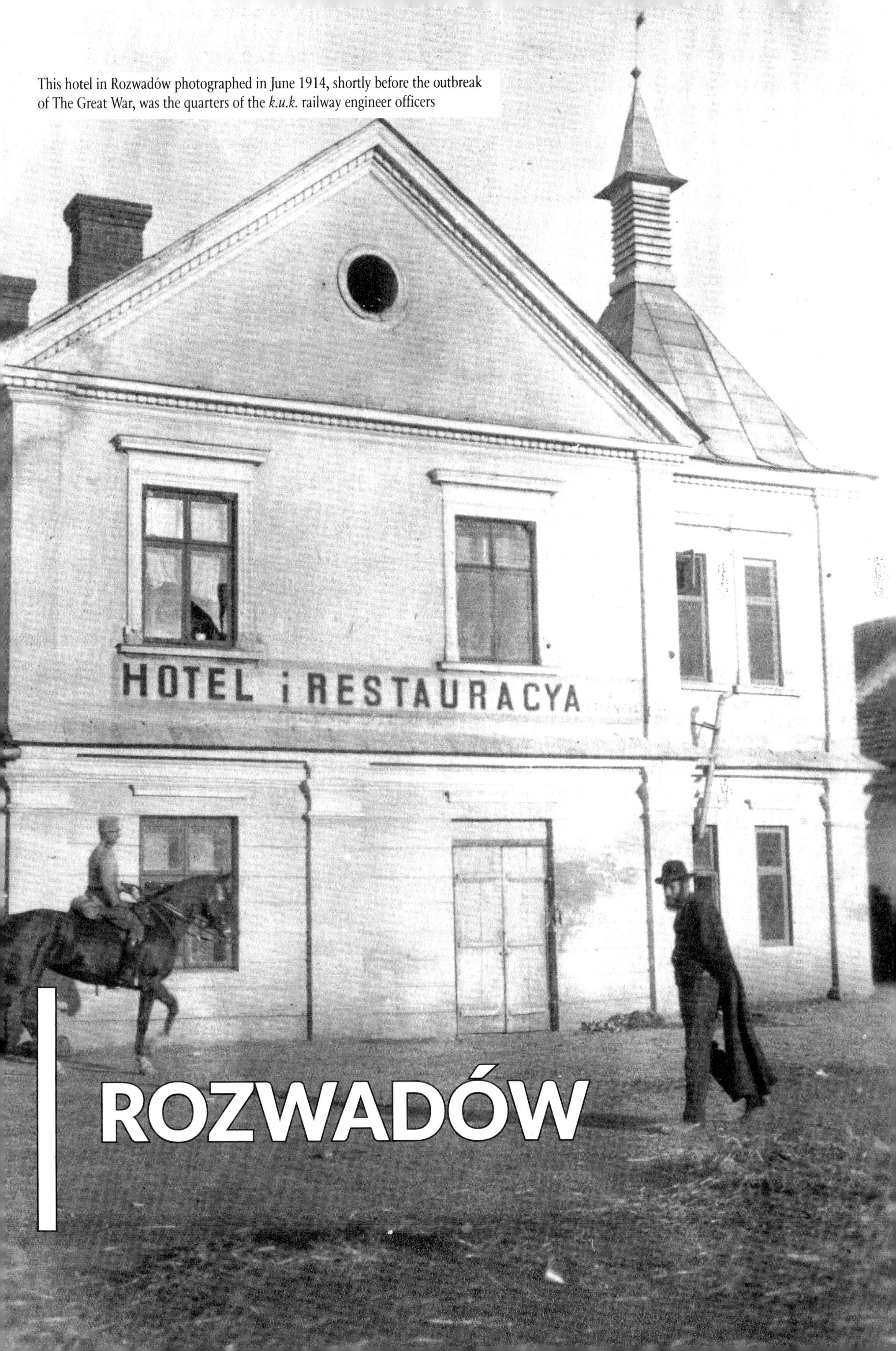


# ROZWADÓW

Market square in Rozwadów crowded with troops, horses and supply carts.

The railway station in Rozwadów. As often, supplies are carried by requisitioned local horse-drawn carts.

Unusual task for the railway engineers – digging trenches near Rozwadów.

The narrow-gauge station in Rozwadów. Note huge amounts of railway sleepers.

The original caption reads: *All obstacles have been removed now*. Indeed, the street seems to be negotiable.

The barbed wire at the border between Galicia and the Russian-held part of Poland near Rozwadów, Autumn 1914.

Mounted troops of the company's supply train section, commanded by Captain-of-Horse Budil, October 1914.

A disassembled mortar transported by the field railway.

**Right:** The same mortar now ready for transport.

**Above:** Early stage of building a bridge over the River San in Rozwadów, June 1915. Engineers of the German *E.B.K. 27.* are commencing to erect a ramp which would run to a bridgehead. The Russians did not have a high, flood-proof bridge at this location. They planned building the bridge and although they had largely finished a part of the ramp which would also act as a dam, most of it was still missing. During their withdrawal, they burnt the supports and elements of the ramp, nevertheless some were re-usable.

**Left:** The first two wooden pillars of the ramp running to the bridgehead have been completed by the Germans of the *E.B.K. 27.*, the third one is under construction. Note the burnt-out elements of the Russian-built ramp which can be seen in the foreground in the lower right part of the image.

**Below:** Once the ramp is ready, the railway engineers can start working on the bridge itself. Note a temporary narrow-gauge transport crossing and two pile drivers, one of which is floating on pontoons.

A part of the ramp or rather a dry gap bridge running to the actual crossing over the River San in Rozwadów under construction, June 1915. The German *E.B.K. 27.* possessed low-support bridge elements, and are now applying parts of the *I-50* type bearers and hammerbeams. We can also see some Austro-Hungarian engineers as the troops of the *2.* and *24. Eisenbahnkompanien* took part in the bridge construction as well. Also two hundred Russian POWs were attached to transport the necessary material.

Captain-of-Horse Budil, the officer commanding of the horse-drawn supply train section.

German railway engineers in the process of construction of the main bridge pillars in the riverbed of San, July 1915. The bridge together with its ramps was completed in eight days.

River San, Rozwadów, July 1915. The first span of the Kohn bridging system is already in place. This means that German engineers have had to familiarize themselves with this Austro-Hungarian solution. We can also see that the hammerbeam had been laid between the two foreground pillars. On the left the bypass narrow-gauge transport crossing is visible, which was depicted in one of the earlier images.

The dry gap part of the bridge is completed, July 1915. Note another narrow-gauge track laid on the ground.

July 1915. Once the bridge is ready it is time for the endurance trials. Here one of them is being performed by a fully-laden train with two locomotives. The leading one is most likely a *kkStB 73* series.

**Left:** A group of *k.u.k.* railway engineers, Summer of 1915.

The entire bridge over River san in Rozwadów is now completed, July 1915. As we said, it took only eight days to build the entire construction of two dry gap ramps and three Kohn system spans.

# ZAKLIKÓW

A railway station in Zaklików, at the Rozwadów-Lublin route, July 1915. The canteen stands were serviced by the local Jewish community. The frontline passed the town three times in 1914 and 1915.

In 1915 Russian engineers built a railway which was to supply their troops fighting in Galicia. They burnt one of their own bridges during the great retreat in 1915. German engineers of the *E.B.K. 17* rebuilt it between 10th and 17th July. It was located in the village of Sanna near Zaklików, now a part of the town.

Austro-Hungarian engineers posing for a photo in Rzeczyca on the Rozwadów-Zaklików route, July 1915. The entire Russian-built railway route had to be narrowed from 1,524 mm gauge to the European 1,435 mm (56.5 in) track spacing.

Sanna bridge, July 1915. First stages of the work – strengthening one of the bridgeheads. German engineers can be seen hand-operating two manual pile drivers.

A field sawmill of the *E.B.K. 17.* preparing material for the Sanna bridge, the bridgehead of which can be seen on the right. A Benz lorry, seen to the left, is powering the sawmill.

The River Sanna bridge and the field sawmill viewed from a slightly different angle. (Mariusz Szewc coll.)

Three manual pile drivers at work in Sanna, July 1915.

The dry gap bridge in Sanny near Zaklików was fully completed on 17 July 1915. The work had been done in seven days.

Work of the E.B.K. 27 is now completed. The Sanna bridge is awaiting an endurance trial. The construction lasted from 10th to 17th July.

The endurance test of the Sanna bridge. The train comprises fully laden tank wagons, including at least two with brakemen's cabs. (Mariusz Szewc coll.)

# KRAŚNIK AREA

**Left:** The war graves in Polankowice, July 1915. An inscription in Cyrillic on the Russian-Orthodox cross reads "Military Brotherly Cemetery".

**Above:** A railway station building in the village of Niedrzwica Mała, July 1915. Note a platform-equipped *kkStB G 73* closed goods wagon.

Niedrzwica Mała, July 1915. The original caption reads *Weiss und Rohne*.

A culvert in Niedrzwica Duża dug in sandy ground under the railway route, built by the *13. Eisenbahnkompanie* entirely of wood, July 1915.

Three views of a damaged church building in Niedrzwica Duża, July 1915.